Whispers
in the
MORNING

A Guide to Discovering God's Voice
in Your Daily Life

TRACY ALAN BARNETT

ISBN: 978-1-7338851-0-2
Library of Congress Control Number: 2019903555

Printed in USA by Tracy Alan Barnett

Photo for Author page by Patrick Dean of Images by Patrick

While all attempts have been made to verify information provided for this publication, the author and publisher assume no responsibility for errors, omissions, or contrary interpretation of the subject matter herein.

For bulk book orders, contact Tracy Alan Barnett, using email address WhsprsMorn@gmail.com.

Dedication

I dedicate this book to my beautiful wife, Carla, without whose support I would be nothing. You continue to encourage me to reach higher and never settle. My sons, Branden and Bryson, who inspire me every day to be a better example. I am so proud to be your dad. To my mother, Alice Asbury, who, before your passing, enjoyed reading and hearing these devotionals, which encouraged you on your journey and battle with cancer. My wonderful mother-in-love, Ms. Lillie McMillon, who inspires me to reach beyond my self-imposed limitation. To all my family and friends, too many to enumerate in this book, thank you for your love and support.

Especially to the "next great generation," the men and women who have sacrificed much to fight the Global War on Terror. Thank you for your sacrifice.

Table of Contents

Introduction

28 October 2009, Camp Egger, Kabul Afghanistan, 0625 AM:

A volley of small arms fire whistling through the streets awakens me like an old friend. The gun battle, right outside the gate, is more reliable than the proverbial rooster trying to wake the sun. No warning comes over the PA system, so I assume we're not under direct attack. As I roll over in bed, I place my hands behind my head like I'm lying in a hammock in the greatest vacation spot ever known to man. I study the ceiling awhile and ponder the situation. Strange what war does to a person. I am eerily at peace listening to this prolonged gun battle, considering the first week when I arrived this very building sustained severe damage when a suicide car bomber detonated his vehicle at the front gate. We lost two soldiers that day: Robinson and Robinson.

Strange what war does to a person. Two people I never met are now indelibly etched in my mind. She was 21 years old with a 2-year-old waiting for her back home, and he was a single father of two and had just two weeks to go before he'd see their faces. With danger all around, fear should have been my constant companion, but after nine months in a warzone I'd grown accustomed to chaos, and fear was kept at bay because my soul was firmly anchored in the Lord.

As I laid in my "hammock," thoughts raced through my head. I wondered if Afghans were fighting each other, or were we sending some home today. I prayed for those that might not see another day, including myself. My family was never far from my mind and heart. Did they know how much love I had for them? Who would care for my boys if I didn't make it home?

The military mission I was here to do was critical, but I knew God had a greater purpose for me, so I asked God, 'why am I here?' I asked God to show me the lesson he wanted to teach me through this experience.

As I uttered those words, He seemed to whisper a scripture to me, *"You will not be afraid of the terror by night, or of the arrow that flies by day;" (Psalms 91:5 NASB).* A peace surrounded me, and I realized even more vividly that God continues to speak to us through His word and in the vibrant colors of our life experiences if we are open to hearing Him.

Since that day, I've intentionally endeavored to open myself to hear the lessons God is showing me through the experiences of my everyday life. I firmly believe God speaks to us through his Word, but He also whispers to us through our problems, through people, and even our pain. Oft times people look for God to answer us in some big way, not realizing that if we take the time to listen, He speaks and reveals Himself in small, intimate whispers.

God has given me a unique gift, borne out of this warzone prayer, to see His hand moving in our daily lives. I share this gift with you now and pray it is a blessing to your life, heart, and spirit.

How to Get the Most Out
of This Guide

This devotional guide is designed as a tool and roadmap to help you begin to hear the whispers in your life. First, I encourage you to read the devotional and reflect on similar experiences you may have faced in your life. Secondly, I encourage you to open your Bible and read the scripture and back story attached to each devotional. Finally, take a moment to write a reflection in the space provided at the end of each chapter, so you can consider how God is speaking to you in your current situation.

I pray as you read and spend more time in God's Word, your faith is increased, and your hope restored. It is my deepest desire that this book helps each of you connect to His purpose and plan for your life. Take time and listen for His "Whispers in the Morning."

Encouragement

Have you ever needed a burst of energy to reach the finish line?

As one of the older cadets in Officer Training School, having already served 15 years in the enlisted corps, there were moments I wanted to quit. This little 5-foot 2-inch lieutenant noticed me slowing down on our final run required for commissioning. Lt. Webb ran beside me and said, "Don't you quit on me! Picture your wife and son at the end of that finish line and keep running."

She gave me the burst of energy I needed to make it to the finish line. May this chapter provide you with that burst of energy needed to keep running.

CHAPTER 1

Whispers of Encouragement

Meet Me at the Tree

"The God of our fathers raised up Jesus whom you murdered by hanging on a tree. Him God has exalted to His right hand to be Prince and Savior, to give repentance to Israel and forgiveness of sins."

Acts 5:30-31

Years ago, when my oldest son started kindergarten, I would walk him to school just about every day. The first week, I would leave him with the same message, "Hey, Daddy loves you and if you ever come out of here and don't see me, just meet me by this tree." I would make him repeat his instructions back to me. I would say, "What are you supposed to do if you don't see daddy?" He would reply, "Meet you at the tree, Dad." The next two weeks, I'd just drop him off and remind him that Daddy loved him. The following week, I wanted to know if he'd heard me, so I stood in a spot where I could see him, but he couldn't see me. What would he do?

Like every other day, he came sprinting out of the door, laughing, jumping, and playing with all the other children. I could see him scanning the schoolyard looking for daddy. When he didn't see me, I could see that momentary panic begin to set in. He started to sprint back toward the school door, and I was a little disappointed... after all that instruction… but then he caught himself, turned, and ran toward the tree. Yes! He had heard my voice. I watched him for a few minutes as he waved goodbye to his friends. I saw him turn down offers to go to the playground. As people asked him questions, I could see him motioning toward the tree, as if to say I'm supposed to be right here.

Listen, I don't know what's going on in your life today, and perhaps you can't see Daddy. Maybe you're lost on the playground of life, but don't panic, don't run in the wrong direction, because Daddy gave us clear instructions. He says to us if we ever get to the place where we can't see Him, all we have to do is meet Him at the tree. You know the tree He is talking about, right? The one on that hill. The hill called Calvary.

IGY6!

"But Abishai son of Zeruiah came to David's rescue; he struck the Philistine down and killed him…"

2 Samuel 21:17

The other day someone asked, "You got my 6?" I instinctively said, "I got it!" The individual was asking if I had his back? If I would protect his blindside? If he could trust me to watch his most vulnerable place for an attack – an area he couldn't see?

We all need someone to get our 6. Ultimately God has our 6, but he puts people in our lives to help us when we feel faint and vulnerable to the enemy's attack. Who has your 6?

I'm glad I have some friends who will check on me now and then and call me out on my mess. We often hear about David and how he slew Goliath, but there was another giant named Ishbi-Benoh.

Here's a quick lesson: Just because you won one scrimmage doesn't mean the war is over.

David felt faint, and this giant was about to spear David to the ground, but David had a friend named Abishai who had his 6. Abishai fought when David couldn't and took down the giant, saving David's life.

Who has your 6? Who's watching that vulnerable part of your life so the enemy doesn't slip into those places you cannot see? Yes, all of us need someone to say, IGY6!

Condition not Conclusion

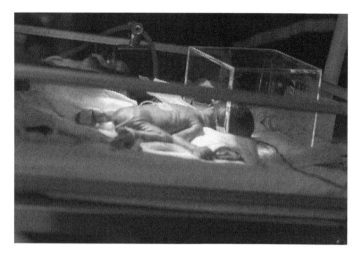

"Now to him who is able to do immeasurably more than all we ask or imagine, according to his power that is at work within us..."

Ephesians 3:20

I heard a mother give a moving testimony about her infant daughter. Her daughter was born with a rare allergic condition that caused her body to reject all food. Can you imagine, your infant child allergic to food or milk? The condition was so serious the doctors recommended the family make final arrangements for the baby girl. The mother prayed and acknowledged the condition, but never believed the condition dictated her daughter's conclusion.

Today, you may feel lonely, overwhelmed, or ready to throw in the towel, but I encourage you, much like this mother, to believe that where you find yourself is only a condition and not your conclusion. Hang in there and wait for your conclusion. God has a way of working all things together for the good. I'm happy to report the infant daughter is now a teenager, and her mother states she can't keep her out of the kitchen.

The Prescription Doesn't
Match My Pain

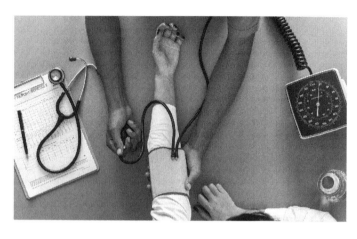

*Naaman's servants went to him and said, "My father,
if the prophet had told you to do some great thing,
would you not have done it? How much more, then,
when he tells you, 'Wash and be cleansed'!"*

2 Kings 5:13

I went to the doctor to have my shoulder
evaluated for the severe pain I had been
experiencing. The pain made it difficult to lift
my arm; I couldn't even get a good night's
sleep. The audible popping that could be
heard clear across the room made me believe
surgery would soon be required. The doctor

did a thorough exam and afterward tossed me a small elastic band, instructing me on some small motion exercises I could use to strengthen the muscle in my shoulder. He assured me if I did the activities, the pain would go away.

Blown away, I was a little confused and frustrated because his prescription did not seem to match my pain. This solution was too simple! He told me, "IF I DID IT" it would work! Similarly, God has given us a prescription that will blow your mind away in its simplicity. He merely asks that you trust, believe, and receive the work He has already done on the cross for you, and he'll take the pain of sin away.

You may think the pain of your past, your heartbreak, your disappointment, is too great even for God, but let me give you a simple motion exercise: Lift your hands and give the problem to Him. In the words of my doctor, it will work, if you do it.

Listen for the Whisper

"After the earthquake came a fire, but the LORD was not in the fire. And after the fire came a gentle whisper."

1 Kings 19:12

We were in Florida on Resurrection Sunday and had the great pleasure of watching some children, dressed in their Sunday best, shake off the nerves to stand tall and recite their Easter speeches. They all did a fantastic job, but two little girls captured my attention. You would have mistaken them for twins if one hadn't stood about six inches taller than the other. I could tell she was the older sister.

They walked to the stage together ready to do their best. The younger sister grabbed the microphone, stood with confidence, but didn't utter a word. The older sister standing close by leaned over to whisper in her ear and then popped back up as if no one could see her. The younger sister repeated every word with boldness as if she'd had her speech memorized for weeks. She blocked out the noise and all the distractions and listened for the whisper.

At times it can be difficult to hear God through all of life's noise and distractions, yet he speaks. These two girls displayed a beautiful picture of how the Holy Spirit wants to work in our lives. He stands in and with us to provide us with the WORD to make it through our test, but we must ignore all of life's noise and listen for that still small voice. So today, I encourage you, much like that younger sister: Listen for His whisper.

G>ΛV

"For behold, He who forms the mountains and creates the wind And declares to man what are His thoughts, He who makes the dawn into darkness And treads on the heights of the earth, The LORD God of hosts is His name."

Amos 4:13

I met a young lady the other day who had a unique tattoo on her arm. As I glanced at it, it looked a little like Greek lettering or symbols, so it caught my attention. I was curious to see if I could read and understand what I assumed was a Greek word written on this young lady's arm.

I wanted to test my skills after spending a bunch of money to learn Greek. After a few seconds, I couldn't crack the code so being the person I am, I naturally had to ask, "What does that tattoo mean?" The tattoo looked a little like this, G>^v, which meant God is greater than my ups and downs. I told her it was a great message and beautiful way for people to ask about the God she served.

As I was leaving, I told her I thought the symbol could also mean, God is greater than my mountains or my valleys. She had never thought about it in that manner but agreed it certainly could be interpreted that way. She said, "In the middle of a hurricane called life, people certainly need to know God is greater than every one of our mountains and every one of our valleys." I know it's tough when we're in the middle of it, but G>^v! Yes, He is!

Personal Reflection

How is God whispering words of encourage-
ment to you today?

_____

_____

_____

_____

_____

_____

_____

_____

_____

What source of strength did God give you the
last time you had a moment of discouragement?
How can you use that today in your current
situation?

_____

_____

_____

_____

_____

_____

_____

_____

_____

HOPE

If God gave you breath in your body, you still have hope.

I've heard it said, "Human beings can live for forty days without food, four days without water, and four minutes without air. But we cannot live for four seconds without hope."

Look, it took you four seconds to read that, which tells me that hope still resides in you.

CHAPTER 2

Whispers of Hope

Living with Urgency

*"As long as it is day, we must do the works
of him who sent me. Night is coming,
when no one can work."*

John 9:4

At age 92, Betty Reid Soskin was the nation's
oldest park ranger. In 2012, Betty worked

at the Rosie the Riveter World War II Home Front National Historical Park in Richmond, CA. In 2012, she was out of work due to the government shutdown. Ranger Betty wanted to get back to teaching park visitors, young and old, how men and women from the segregated South came together to build ships for the war effort.

As the government shutdown ended, Betty, reflecting on the event said, "It was disconcerting because I live with a sense of urgency now. It's a period where if I don't get it right, I don't have time to do it again."

We should all embrace Betty's words, because the truth of the matter is, you don't have to be 92 to understand you might not get another chance to get it right. We are all called to live with a sense of urgency, because we may not see tomorrow.

Jesus is our perfect example of living with a sense of urgency and purpose. Jesus in attending to the needs of a blind man said, "I must work the works of Him who sent Me while it is day; [the] night is coming when no one can work..."

Like Betty, and much more like Jesus, we must understand our time is limited and we must live with a sense of urgency. So today, live to forgive someone, tell someone you love them, share your testimony, or share the gospel. My mother would say it this way: "This may be the last time, I don't know." Today, live with urgency for it may be our last time to get it right.

Winners!!!

"I have fought the good fight, I have finished the race, I have kept the faith. Now there is in store for me the crown of righteousness, which the Lord, the righteous Judge, will award to me on that day— and not only to me, but also to all who have longed for his appearing."

2 Timothy 4:7-8

I met a man the other day whose son is "mentally challenged," but he shared with me, every day his son teaches him some of life's greatest lessons. He shared one of those lessons with me. His son was running the

100-yard dash in the Special Olympics when one of his competitors slipped and fell. His son and the other individuals in the race all stopped and went back to pick up the one who fell. The crowd stood in stunned silence as they all crossed the line together, lifted their hands and shouted at the top of their voices, "WINNERS!!!"

I am often amazed at how the ones we label as "challenged" can teach all of us. Through their actions, these children taught us a beautiful life lesson. We're all in the race together, but we're not competing against one another. Now and then, just like these children, we must stop to help someone get back up and finish this course. This race is not a competition where one person must lose for the other to win, but more about our capacity for compassion where we all claim victory. If we help one another along the way, we'll cross the finish line together to lift our hands and our voices to shout…WINNERS!

I Found Another Penny!

"And when she has found it, she calls her friends and neighbors together, saying, 'Rejoice with me, for I have found the piece which I lost!' Likewise, I say to you, there is joy in the presence of the angels of God over one sinner who repents."

Luke 15: 9-10

Oh look, found another one! It never ceases to amaze me, but just about every time my wife and I take a jog around the neighborhood, we find some change. It could be a penny here or a nickel, dime, or quarter there, but we usually find something. I don't know if the coins were accidentally dropped or intentionally discarded, but when we come across them, we'll pick them up, because they're worth something.

You can tell by the condition of some of the coins that they've been in the elements for a while. Some are dirty, some are bent, some walked on, or flattened by cars, but we'll still pick them up because regardless of the condition, the coins still have not lost their value.

Have you ever felt like a lost coin? Perhaps someone accidentally dropped you or intentionally discarded you, and made you feel less than worthy. I'm writing to remind you, God has placed great value in you and still sees you as having great worth.

God made you in his very image, and no matter how long you've been in the elements, no matter how dirty or beaten you feel, God is still looking for you to pick you up! He'll pick you up, clean you off, and cause you to shine again because you have not lost your value.

Do you know His Voice?

"My sheep hear My voice, and I know them,
and they follow Me."

John 10:27

As a child, we'd play outside all day. The general rule was to be home before the street lights came on. On those rare occasions when parents needed to reach their children before the street light curfew, they would stand at the front door and yell their name.

When I was growing up, we didn't have cell phones, so the agreed upon form of communication in the neighborhood was the yell phone.

Somehow, the shouting voice of my mother would always seem to find me. I could pick out her voice from the noise and all the other voices because I knew her voice.

Well, in a similar way, we must know God's voice. Today, there is so much noise and other voices that it can be difficult to hear God calling you. To cut through the noise, we must spend time in prayer and reading His word to grow familiar with the tone of his voice. It's getting late, and He's calling your name. Why don't you answer His call?

Move Forward

"Now the LORD had said to Abram, Get you out of your country, and from your kindred, and from your father's house, to a land that I will show you."

Genesis 12:1

Have you ever missed your signal to move forward? I admit there have been times I missed my green light because I had some deep thought at the light. Someone watching me had to blow their horn to remind me it was my time to move forward.

Well, our lives can be a little like this at times. We can become so engaged or distracted by the cares of this life that we can miss God's green light. As this week comes to a close, think about those dreams and visions God gave you so many years ago, and ask yourself, "Why am I still sitting at this intersection? Is it time to move forward?"

I merely showed up today to blow my horn to tell you the light is green, God is with you, and it's time to move forward in the things God has purposed in your life. It is not too late. Move forward!

Putting Your Little in His Hands

"Taking the five loaves and the two fish and looking up to heaven, he gave thanks and broke them. Then he gave them to the disciples to distribute to the people. They all ate and were satisfied, and the disciples picked up twelve basketfuls of broken pieces that were left over."

Luke 9:16-17

I was reflecting on my mother and how she always had a meal ready for us to eat. I can't remember a day I had to go hungry, but I do remember days when I'd walked into the kitchen, looked through the cabinets, and not seen much food in the house.

My mother would walk into the same kitchen and see the same emptiness, but then she would say these words, "Father I stretch my hands to thee; no other help I know. If thou withdraw thyself from me, wherever shall I go?"

It seemed that by the time she uttered that simple prayer and thanked God for the little we had, the aroma of our next meal would fill the house. Somehow, she turned what little we had into a meal that fed everyone, and yes there were leftovers.

I don't know what you're going through today. It may feel like what you have is not enough. You may even feel like you're not enough, but I dare you to put the little you have in God's hand. What little you have in His hand is much greater than you think.

Personal Reflection

What word of hope is God whispering to you today?

_____

_____

_____

_____

_____

_____

_____

_____

_____

What is the source of your hope? How do you maintain it?

_____

_____

_____

_____

_____

_____

_____

_____

_____

_____

LONELY

You are not alone.

Sometimes, we need to remind ourselves when loneliness tries to overwhelm our heart to let God into the situation.

Someone said, "The ones who notice the storms in your eyes, the silence in your voice, and the heaviness in your heart are the ones you need to let in."

God notices. Let Him in.

CHAPTER 3

Whispers for the Lonely

Beyond the Bend

"Have I not commanded you? Be strong and courageous. Do not be frightened, and do not be dismayed, for the Lord your God is with you wherever you go."

Joshua 1:9

Not long ago, I had a moment to take a walk-in silent prayer. It was an opportunity to tune out all the distraction from the day with no headphones, no telephone, and no emails. Just allowing the Lord to speak to me.

As I walked through the wooded trail, the path turned, and I had no idea what awaited me around the bend. Not knowing can make a person apprehensive, and sometimes you might even want to turn around, but here's what I have discovered: Your blessing might be right around the bend.

Amid this apprehension, I had an overwhelming sense of peace. I knew that God was not only walking with me, but He was already beyond the bend making provision, smoothing my path, and taking care of any would-be enemy.

Listen, I don't know what's beyond the bend in your life, but God is not only with you, He is beyond that bend making a way just for you. Don't give up. Don't stop walking. Don't turn around. I believe your blessing is right around the bend. Trust God and keep walking.

Blessed, but in Despair

"He has delivered us from such a deadly peril, and he will deliver us again. On him we have set our hope that he will continue to deliver us,"

2 Corinthians 1:10

Every day I'm privileged to minister to people, in the words of Apostle Paul, burdened beyond their strength so that they despair for life itself. Paul, speaking about the trouble in his life declared it felt like a death sentence (2 Cor 1: 8-11).

Perhaps you can identify with Paul. Maybe life's trouble has hit you like a ton of bricks, and your strength is almost gone, and your despair feels overwhelming. Well, Paul helps us understand difficulty is not uncommon. Yes, you can be "blessed and highly favored," and still walk in despair.

Life is hard. I need to say that because there are some who may believe something is wrong with them or their faith because trouble has knocked on their door. If Paul is an example to us, he teaches us how to respond to stress.

First, he acknowledged the reality of his hurt. He claimed it so that God could heal it. Secondly, he accepted his limitations to fix the issue. Paul realized the trouble was beyond his strength, but never beyond God's. Third, he recognized the power of prayer. Paul not only called on God, but a community of people prayed for and with him, and their prayers moved heaven and encouraged Paul. Finally, he found a purpose in his pain. His pain led him to have greater compassion for others.

I have often been asked, "How do you deal with the heaviness of others' burdens all day?" What a great question. I thought about it for a moment and said, "I find the joy in the moment, I learn to laugh and act a fool, and I look for the light in the dark place" (Jesus is the light). I understand while I am leading others in prayer today, like Paul, I may need someone to help me see the light tomorrow. Hang on, you will make it if you continue to walk toward the light.

A Childlike Faith

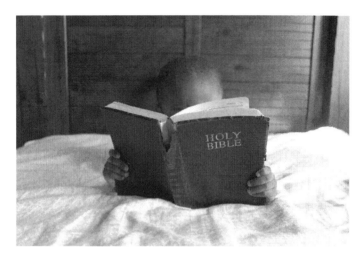

"Assuredly, I say to you, whoever does not receive the kingdom of God as a child will by no means enter it."

Mark 10:15

Many years ago, as a child, I prayed a simple prayer of faith, and accepted Christ as my Savior and asked him to be Lord of my life. Whatever he wanted me to do, go, or say, I was committed to doing it. He was and continues to be Lord of my life.

Did I understand everything? No. I still don't understand everything. In the words of an old gospel song, "I don't know why he loves me. I don't know why he cares. I don't know why he sacrificed his life, but I'm glad, so very glad he did."

I'm also glad God does not require a child to understand like an adult. But you know, He does require an adult to believe as a child. Jesus said, "Assuredly, I say to you, whoever does not receive the kingdom of God as a child will by no means enter it" (Mark 10:15).

So today, I urge you, like a parent encouraging their child to take that first step of faith, to trust God and know he'll catch you just like a loving parent. I urge you, in these challenging times, (for my poker fans) to go all in for Christ. Trust Him! If you're glad that God heard your simple prayer, you should take a minute and give God the highest praise!

Anything for My Daddy

"For whoever is ashamed of Me and My words, of him, the Son of Man will be ashamed when He comes in His glory, and in His Father's, and of the holy angels"

(Luke 9:26)."

"My dad has been out of a job for three years, and I wanted to give you his resume," said ten-year-old Charlotte Bell. Typically, these words may have gone unnoticed, but she asked the right person and brought attention to her family's condition. Charlotte asked the First Lady of the United States to take her father's resume. Stunned and touched, Ms. Obama wrapped her arms around the young girl to comfort her.

I will not argue if her actions were appropriate, but I do admire Charlotte's boldness. She was willing to go to the highest authority she could think of to advocate for her father. She was willing to risk embarrassment, rejection, reputation, and scorn from the media and teasing from her friends. She did it all for her daddy. I am sure she thought this would please her father and help him on his mission to find a job.

Well, I wonder if we have such boldness for our Heavenly Father.

Are we willing to stand and call attention to our Father, and risk embarrassment, rejection, reputation, the scorn and ridicule of the world? Young Ms. Charlotte was determined to do anything for her daddy. Are you? Sometimes, we must be willing to take a risk and do anything for Daddy.

Run Easy

"…let us run with endurance the race that is set before us…"

Hebrews 12:1

I found out it's much easier to run when your mind is on God's favor. On a frigid morning, I shook myself awake to go out for a quick run, but my mouth was full of complaints. My list of complaints was endless: It's too dark, it's too cold, I'm too old for this stuff, my knees hurt, my back hurts, and on and on. It was slow treading the first mile, but I dragged myself through it, talking myself out of quitting several times. It was the worst run I could remember in a long time, but something changed at the mile marker.

At the mile marker, I spotted a person on the running path in front of me. As I thought about it, I realized he had gotten up earlier than I did and started before me. It was colder and darker when he began, and the place he'd reached on the path was more difficult for him than for me. You see, the person on the path was in a wheelchair. Instantly my attitude and focus changed when I spotted him. I noticed as I jogged beside him, his legs were amputated above the thigh, and yet here he was up early on a cold morning seemingly without complaint.

The next two miles became easier because my complaints turned to praise. Lord, Thank You…for the pains in my knees! Lord, Thank You…that I'm able to feel the cold on my face! Lord, Thank You…for letting me see you erase the darkness from the sky! Lord, Thank You…for allowing me to see the sunrise this morning! Lord, Thank You…for giving me the energy to run at this age! The final miles flew by because I didn't focus on self, but I focused on His goodness.

How's your run going? Let me encourage you; the journey becomes much easier when you have a mind to praise Him for everything instead of complaining about small things, and everything is small when compared to the God we serve.

A Shepherd's Love

"He tends his flock like a shepherd: He gathers the lambs in his arms and carries them close to his heart, and he gently leads those that have young."

Isaiah 40:11

Scripture always reminds us of God's great love towards us. In the book of Isaiah, we read how He will tend to us, which means He'll provide for or feed us. Not only will He provide for us, but He protects us. He will embrace you in His arms. There's no better place to be than in the arms of the Lord. There is safety in His arms. Third, when we feel like we can't go another step, the scripture says He'll carry us. Has the Lord ever had to carry you? Finally, as the Good Shepherd, He will lead us in the right direction. Trust His leadership and direction, and you will end up in the right place. He is the Good Shepherd, and he cares for us.

We have a Good Shepherd, and no matter what you may face this week, remember God cares. Isaiah shares four promises about the Shepherd's love that you should tuck away in your heart. Let Isaiah's four promises concerning the love of our Shepherd guide your steps, speech, and heart as you go through your week.

Personal Reflection

How is God whispering to you in these
moments of loneliness?

_____

_____

_____

_____

_____

_____

_____

_____

_____

_____

_____

_____

_____

_____

_____

_____

_____

_____

_____

_____

_____

_____

Who has He put in your path to encourage you?

_____

_____

_____

_____

_____

_____

_____

_____

_____

_____

_____

_____

_____

_____

_____

_____

_____

_____

_____

_____

_____

BROKEN

Sorrow visits all of us. The scripture reminds us that, "Weeping may endure a night," because this life has heartbreaking and painful moments. I know, I've had a few.

The good news is we don't have to walk through this sadness alone. God is the God of all comfort, and he promised to be with us even through life's most difficult moments.

Jesus said He came to heal the brokenhearted, which includes you and me.

Chapter 4

Whispers for the Broken

You're in His Hand

"Look, as the clay is in the potter's hand,
so are you in My hand…"

Jeremiah 18:6

Have you ever dropped a dish and it broke into several pieces? I have and it's always frustrating. Your favorite dish now on the ground in several pieces. What to do? A reasonable person would sweep it up and throw it out. I mean, you really can't do much with broken stuff, or can you?

A Japanese art form, called Kintsugi, declares there is a lot you can do with broken stuff. A Kintsugi artist would take that broken dish and restore it by pouring a special lacquer dusted with powdered gold, silver, or platinum into the damaged areas. Beautiful streams of gold glint would fill the cracks of ceramic ware, giving a unique appearance to the piece. The gold highlights the places where the pottery had been cracked, broken, or damaged.

The artist does not try to hide, cover, or disguise the cracks or the flaws in the pottery. On the contrary, they highlight those flaws, because when the potter restores the pottery, it is the flaws that demonstrate the potter's ability to bring beauty out of brokenness.

Scripture tells us the word of the Lord came to a prophet named Jeremiah. Jeremiah was told to go down to a potter's house where he would hear a word from the Lord. When Jeremiah arrived at the potter's house, he saw a vessel made of clay on the wheel, but it was damaged, so the potter remade it into another vessel, and it pleased the potter.

The Lord asked this question of Jeremiah. "Can I not deal with you and my people as this potter does with the clay?" The Lord declared, "Behold, like the clay in the potter's hand, so are you in My hand." Can I ask the same question of you today? Can God make you over? Yes, He can!

All of us have some cracks, but I dare you to let God pour His Spirit into you and put you on display. We often hesitate to be on display, but the cracks in our lives demonstrate the work the master potter has done.

Broken Places

"He heals the brokenhearted and binds up their wounds."

Psalm 147:3

The other day I had a conversation with a Physical Therapist, and she talked about how broken bones heal. She explained how collagen forms around the fracture, and for a brief period in the healing process, the fractured site is stronger than the surrounding bone.

Ernest Hemingway once famously wrote, "The world breaks everyone, and afterward many are strong at the broken places." Have you ever been in a broken place? I'm confident you have because we're all broken in one way or another. A quick scan of our world and you'll notice brokenness all around: broken marriages, broken families, broken relationships, and hurting, brokenhearted people just about everywhere.

We usually try to rid ourselves of broken things as quickly as possible, but for some reason, God sees some beauty in our brokenness and wants to keep us. Scripture tells us in Psalm 34:18, "The Lord is near to the brokenhearted and saves the crushed in spirit." We have this promise in Psalm 147:3, "He heals the brokenhearted and binds up their wounds."

When the Lord binds our wounds, it means we are in the middle of our healing process, and as a therapist reminded me, it means we are getting stronger in that broken place. Listen, I don't know what you're going through today, but encourage yourself and others and shout, "STRONGER," because that's what you'll be AFTER THIS.

Cracks in the Wall

"…for all have sinned and fall short of the glory of God, being justified freely by His grace through the redemption that is in Christ Jesus…"

Rom 3:23-24

I was in a building the other day, and I noticed many cracks that ran down the walls. Over the years, the ground underneath the building probably shifted causing the cracks in the walls. The cracks were so large I could see the sunlight shining on the other side of the wall. The wall didn't look very nice, to be honest, it was kind of ugly, but it helped me see my own life.

I had to admit, as will you if you're honest with yourself, we all have some cracks in our lives. We have some places in our lives, under close inspection, that don't look that good, and we might call it ugly. Have you ever had a time in your life where the ground shifted underneath you, and life gave you some cracks?

As I consider it, I'm okay with my cracks, my flaws, my imperfections, because my cracks allow the SON to shine into my life, and when I walk into a dark place people can see the light inside that comes pouring out of my life because of the cracks.

We are imperfect people who serve a perfect God. Somebody should be rejoicing right now because your cracks didn't disqualify you from being used by God. Cracked, but still worthy! Worthy of His grace, worthy of His mercy, worthy of His love!

Who Broke This?

"The sacrifices of God are a broken spirit; a broken and a contrite heart, O God You will not despise."

Psalm 51:17

Typically, there's always something broken around my house, and the funny thing is the same person is always to blame: "I don't know." *I don't know* has broken just about everything in my house. As parents, we have come to understand that dealing with broken things is all a part of life.

One theologian makes this observation: "Broken things are often useless, but some things need to be broken before they are useful." He writes, "A farmer doesn't plant his crop in cement, but he chooses good soil, breaks it up, and then sows the seed. Unbroken soil does not produce abundant crops, but cultivated soil nurtures life. Jesus did not feed the five thousand until he broke the bread (Mark 8:1–8). The sinful woman could not pour the costly perfume over Jesus until she broke the alabaster box (Luke 7:37). God could not reconcile Himself to sinful man until he broke down the wall that separated us and Him (Ephesians 2:14). We can never know salvation without Jesus' broken body (1 Corinthians 11:24)."

David wrote, "The sacrifice you want is a broken spirit. A broken and repentant heart, O God, you will not despise" (Psalm 51:17 NLT). Today you may feel overwhelmed by things you are facing or even broken by issues of the past, but God does not make mistakes. So, I can say with great confidence, watch God bring life out of that broken place.

You are not alone. We all suffer from some brokenness in our lives, but when we are honest with God and trust Him, He will turn the thing that tried to break us into a blessing for others. God will use the fractured pieces of our lives to speak hope to someone, comfort a hurting soul, and ultimately bring glory to His name.

Two Words Could Fix It

"Our foolish pride comes from this world, and so do our selfish desires and our desire to have everything we see. None of this comes from the Father."

John 2:16 (CEV)

I have seen some sad things in my life, but there's nothing sadder than sitting by the bedside of a person, soon to leave this earth, and they have no one who knows them personally at their side in their last moments. They long for their children or a loved one that they'd lost contact with many years ago because somehow their pride got in the way.

As I talk with them, the regret of the lost relationship fills the room like an unwanted guest. Often, they can't remember how or why the relationship ended, which makes the situation worst. For those who can recall the reason, at that moment, they realize it wasn't worth it. The saddest moment of all is when they understand they could have fixed the relationship long ago with two words: I'm sorry.

I've found that just two words could fix a whole lot of problems if you use them. Have you tried these two words: I'm sorry, or forgive me, or love you, how about...my bad? Today, I pray you're not letting pride and two little words get in the way of a relationship that was meant to bless you.

The funny thing is two words could also fix your relationship with God. It's not hard. He made it easy for us to have a relationship with Him. I dare you to tell the Lord, I'm sorry, or forgive me, or love you, or my bad, better yet, Save Me! These two words could fix it if you don't let your pride get in the way.

Show Me Where It Hurts

"He himself bore our sins" in his body on the cross, so that we might die to sins and live for righteousness; "by his wounds you have been healed."

1 Peter 2:24

As a father of two boys, believe me, I've seen my share of cuts and bruises. It's funny though, the worse the injury, the more they'd resist showing me where it hurt. The pain was so severe that they would rather hold it to themselves than to have me to look at it. I understood their pain, but I couldn't help them until they showed me the wound, no matter how ugly. Sometimes, I would practically have to wrestle them to see their injuries. The pain made them misunderstand that Daddy was there to help them, not hurt them even more. I would finally say to them, "Listen, if you want it to get better, you have to show me where it hurts."

In the same way, living in this world, we will have some hurts. The pain can be so overwhelming that we'll hold on to it for years, thinking time will make it better. What we discover is that an untreated wound can get infected and affect other areas of our lives.

I know you don't want anyone to look at your wound because it hurts too much! But God can heal your pain and bind up your wounds. You have to show Him where it hurts and ask God to heal your wound. No matter how ugly the wound may be, He is able to heal your pain.

Personal Reflection

What is God whispering to you concerning your brokenness?

_____

_____

_____

_____

_____

_____

_____

_____

_____

_____

_____

_____

_____

_____

_____

_____

_____

_____

_____

_____

_____

_____

How has God helped you to mend from the hurt of the past?

_____

_____

_____

_____

_____

_____

_____

_____

_____

_____

_____

_____

_____

_____

_____

_____

_____

_____

_____

_____

_____

_____

_____

JOY

D o you ever feel stuck in the sorrow that surrounds you?

The Psalmist, in completing his thought concerning grief, declares, "Joy comes in the morning (Psalms 30:5)."

One way we can rediscover our joy is to look for it in the so-called "small" things we experience every day. This can move us from a place of despair to a place of healing and gratitude for our joy in the Lord.

CHAPTER 5

Whispers of Joy

Daily Bread and Daily Mercy

"Through the Lord's mercies, we are not consumed, Because His compassions fail not. They are new every morning; Great is Your faithfulness."

Lamentations 3: 22-23

Years ago, my wife and I lived in Mons, Belgium. In the village, there was a small bakery filled with some of the most spectacularly decorated cakes and pies one might imagine, but it was best known for its bread. The smell of freshly baked bread filled the air every morning, and the aroma piqued our curiosity and pulled us inside the quaint little shop.

They greeted all their customers by singing, "Bonjour," like it was the first time they ever saw them. We quickly discovered the small bakery was a staple in the community. Everyone seemed to know the bakers personally, and the bakers seemed to know you because they saw everyone just about every day. You see, the small freshly baked loaves of bread were just enough for that day or that meal, and they planned to sing, "Bonjour" to you all over again the next day.

Well, much like that Belgium bread, God's mercy is new every morning. The aroma of His mercy fills the air and every day, He invites us to know Him in a real and personal way. We used yesterday's mercy yesterday, and God wants to sing, "Bonjour" to you this morning. Have you stopped by the bakery? Have you had a chance to tell the Baker thank you for fresh mercy this morning?

It's in the Basket

"And we know that all things work together for good to those who love God, to those who are the called according to His purpose."

Romans 8:28

My wife loves watching the Food Network, especially some of the cooking competitions. Okay, I sneak a peek at a couple of them myself. On one show, they provide a basket of secret ingredients, and the cook must figure out how to take these surprise ingredients and turn it into something eatable. The basket items are often strange, nasty and bitter, and substances you would never eat alone, but mixed with the other ingredients in the basket they're able to turn it into something good.

Well, life is a little like this cooking show. There are some ingredients in our basket we'd rather not deal with and can't understand why we have them in the first place. Why is this disappointment in my basket? I know I didn't need this sadness, but it's in my basket. Really? Why is this heartbreak in my basket? Somehow, all of this, mixed with God's grace can turn out for good.

I believe God's word is true when the scripture says, "And we know that all things work together for good to those who love God, to those who are the called according to His purpose." It doesn't say everything is always good, but it says whatever you're experiencing it is working for good. Hang in there. It will get better. Trust God enough to know it is working!

Visual Lethargy

"Let all the earth fear the Lord; Let all the inhabitants of the world stand in awe of Him."

Psalms 33:8

I was reading this morning about visual lethargy, which means the more you see something, the less of it you actually see. Artists guard against visual lethargy to capture the beauty on their canvass that most people overlook.

I think we all suffer from a little visual lethargy from time to time, and we miss the beauty that surrounds us every day. We get comfortable and overlook the beauty of a flower or song of a small bird, or the smile of the one you married years ago. The more we see, the less we see. Like an artist, we must intentionally guard against visual lethargy in our relationship with the Lord.

Sometimes we grow so comfortable with the Lord that we are no longer in awe of Him. We are so casual with His grace that we are no longer amazed by it. There is a great danger in losing our awe for God because it motivates everything we do. I love you the way I do because I stand in awe of an Almighty God.

The awe of God should lift you out of dark moments and discouragement. The awe of God is the source of celebration. Don't lose your awe! Today open the eyes of your heart and stand in awe of the Lord once again. Lord, every day I will bless your name because I am in awe of you.

Great Treasure

*"But from there you will seek the L*ORD* your God, and you will find Him if you search for Him with all your heart and all your soul."*

Deuteronomy 4:29

I was at the beach the other day and noticed a man with a metal detector searching diligently for buried treasure. He was so focused on finding a precious coin that he blocked out everything else to listen to his machine indicate that something of great value was near.

Now, I never saw him find anything, but I can imagine if he had found something, he'd want everyone to know of his great fortune. Well, what we have in the Lord is better than any precious coin or metal you could ever find.

In the Lord, we've found the treasure of His love, peace, and forgiveness. We are compelled to tell everybody of our great treasure because of the overwhelming joy of our salvation. Is your detector working? There is still great treasure in the Lord waiting just for you.

You Got that Mark!

"But you are a chosen generation,
a royal priesthood, a holy nation,
His own special people…"

1 Peter 2:9

Reverend Williams, a 97-year-old African-American, World War II Veteran, walked the hospital hallway the other day. He was dressed in his black suit with his white shirt and black tie, topping it off with a black fedora on his head. In my mind, I assumed he dressed this way every day considering it was about 90 degrees in the Florida heat. He held his cane to steady his balance but walked at a good pace. As he walked, he spotted me at some distance coming in the opposite direction. He waved me over, and said, "You're a preacher, aren't you?" I replied, "Well, yes sir, I am. I'm the Chaplain for this hospital."

He said, "I knew it. You've got the mark on you. I never miss a mark. I know a preacher when I see one." Now I must confess I don't know what he saw, discerned, or perceived, but he knew there was something that distinguished me from the rest of the crowd. I'm grateful this man spotted something in me that made him stop to remind me I should never try to blend in with the crowd.

God has called us to stand out from the crowd. He uses us as a light in dark places. God calls us to be extraordinarily different. The Bible says in 1 Peter 2:9, "But you are a chosen generation, a royal priesthood, a holy nation, His own special people, that you may proclaim the praises of Him who called you out of darkness into the marvelous light..."

To me, it sounds like people should always see a distinguishing mark on your life because when we are born-again, we are innately different. So, stop trying to fit into places where you don't belong, and stop trying to hide, because the mark is on you.

Personal Reflection

Consider the most joyful moments in your life.

What is God whispering to you about them right now?

_____

_____

_____

_____

_____

_____

_____

_____

_____

When you close your eyes and think of joy, what do you see yourself doing? How can you experience some of that today?

_____

_____

_____

_____

_____

_____

_____

_____

_____

PRAISE

Praise is a natural expression and the outpouring of joy that is within us.

The Psalmist writes, "The LORD is great and is to be highly praised; His greatness is beyond understanding."

Praise is a recognition that it is only by the grace of God that we live, move, and have our being.

May we stand in awe of God's power, love, and authority in our lives.

Chapter 6

Whispers of Praise

A Super Bloom

"Yea, though I walk through the valley of the shadow of death, I will fear no evil; For You are with me; Your rod and Your staff, they comfort me…"

Psalms 23:4

Life in Death Valley. My wife and I were watching the news last night and noticed how the world stopped to admire a once-in-a-decade event. A rare "super bloom" in the middle of the hottest and driest place in North America, Death Valley, caused people to stand still and take notice. Watching the news, my wife saw the event through a spiritual eye and said that's a word for today. She knew there was something different about a desert exploding with the color of life as flowers covered the desert floor. So, I took notice.

The news anchor, in explaining the story said, "It takes the right circumstances for a 'super bloom' to happen." He shared how seeds coated the desert floor for years, but it needed the right amount of rain for the bloom to occur, and the previous year they'd had significant storms. The storms moved rocks, uncovered the seed, and loosened the hard places so that the flowers could grow.

Have you ever wondered why you have been in the storm so long? Could it be that God is getting you ready for a super bloom? If you ever felt like you were in a desert place and nothing would grow, I want to encourage you today to never underestimate the seed

God has placed in your life. The rain in your life just might move some rocks, uncover seeds, and loosen some rough places for growth.

When God gets finished, the world will marvel at how you can bloom in the middle of your Death Valley! I dare you to find someone today and tell them, "Just watch me bloom!" Tell them, "I know you can't see it right now because of all of that rain and hail in my life but watch me bloom!"

The Walk

Now the sun rose upon him just as he crossed over Penuel, and he was limping on his thigh."

Genesis 32:31

Someone once observed of me, "You got this cool kinda swagger when you walk." Now, I'm not sure I agree, and I'm not co-signing to this person's opinion. However, I thought it was an interesting observation, and it taught me a couple of things.

First, if people are observing my physical walk then more than likely they're observing my spiritual walk. It made me a little more aware that my walk, as a believer, is under constant observation.

Secondly, people aren't always aware of what you've gone through to get your walk. Doctors have said I have no cartilage left in either knee, just bone rubbing on bone... painful. Not long ago I could barely walk up a flight of stairs, but by grace here I am still walking.

From afar, it may look like swagger, but it might just be the residue of struggle and pain. Well, two things changed my walk: my encounter with pain, and my encounter with the Healer. Let me encourage you today. I know it's painful, but God is working on your walk, so one day someone may see it and call it swagger.

When the Battle Shows Up at Lunchtime

"...And Saul said to David, "Go, and the Lord be with you!"

1 Samuel 7:37

I have discovered that sometimes the battle shows up at lunchtime. I mean, when you left this morning, you had no idea you would be entering a fight, but here it is.

David, a shepherd boy, left one morning carrying lunch to his brothers and found himself in a fight. He went out as a shepherd and came back a warrior because the battle showed up at lunchtime.

Sometimes the challenge in our lives comes when we least expect it. You didn't expect those results from the doctor, but here it is. You didn't see that person hurting you, nor that one leaving you, but here it is. What do you do when the battle shows up at lunchtime?

We learn a few lessons from David's experience. First, you are prepared for the battle, because God has already brought you through other problems that were as terrifying as lions and bears.

Second, don't change your practice. David had a habit of relying on the Lord to bring him through each challenge in his life, and his habit didn't change when he faced this new giant.

Third, understand there's a purpose for this battle. David's goal, as should be ours, was to glorify the God he served. We didn't ask for this fight, but we can declare like David; we come to this lunchroom in the name of the Lord for the battle is His, and He will prevail. You've got this!

Drifting

"Enter by the narrow gate; for wide is the gate and broad is the way that leads to destruction, and there are many who go in by it. Because narrow is the gate and difficult is the way which leads to life, and there are few who find it."

Matthew 7:13-14

I've reached that point in life that most parents fear: teaching their child to drive. My son is a pretty good driver, but I've had moments where I've seen my life flash before my eyes. One thing my wife has noticed is at times he drifts into the other lane and, now and then, we'll hear her panicked voice yell, "You're drifting!" He quickly adjusts the wheel and gets back on course. There is a danger in drifting.

Have you ever found yourself drifting? God has put you on a particular path, and for some reasons you find yourself drifting away from the course set by God. Why do we drift? Perhaps you're like my son, and you start to look at the things on the side of the road; or could it be we're trying to keep up with the flow of traffic (world) around us, and we slowly move away from God's direction?

We drift from our homes, our marriages, and in our commitments to Him. If we keep drifting away from God, eventually we will end up crashing. When we drift away from God's direction, it will always end in destruction. So, let me yell in my most panicked voice hoping that you will quickly adjust to His Will, "You're drifting!"

Restored

"...O God, You have cast us off; You have broken us down; You have been displeased; Oh, restore us again!"

Psalms 60:1

My wife brought home some old bookcases and shelves she'd picked up from a second-hand store. She thought they were "perfect" and just needed a little work, but I didn't see any redeeming quality in the items. She saw what they could be, but all I saw is what they were at that moment, "junk."

She stripped, sanded, cleaned them up and put a new finish on them. They looked brand new. She restored them and gave them a brand-new purpose and proved me wrong once again.

Our lives can sometimes resemble an old bookcase or shelf. Beaten, battered and thrown away by others, but thank God he knows how to restore us. Won't He do it! We sometimes look at our lives at the moment, but God sees us through eternity and knows all that we will be. He'll bring you into the house, clean you up, and give you a brand-new purpose. Trust Him.

Do You Have the Right Training?

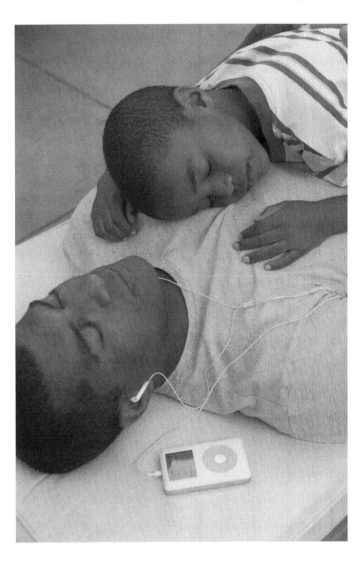

"I hear the tumult of the raging seas as your waves and surging tides sweep over me. But each day the LORD pours his unfailing love upon me, and through each night I sing his songs, praying to God who gives me life."

Psalm 42:7- 8 NLT

In 2014, nine-year-old Willie Myrick was kidnapped from his southwest Atlanta driveway. I can't imagine how terrifying this was for him and his parents. What do you do when the terror of this life tries to overcome you? What do you do in those emergency situations when you have no idea how things will turn out? As a military man, I've learned that in emergency situations most people will do what they've been trained to do. In training, you develop certain habits and they become second nature, so in times of stress you'll do what comes naturally.

Willie did what he was trained to do. During this terrifying ordeal, Willie began to sing a gospel song. Willie loved gospel music, and one reporter wrote, "It may have been his love for the gospel music that saved his life." I will go one further than the reporter; it may have been his love for the Lord that saved his life that day.

You see, when the kidnapper pulled Willie into the car, Willie began singing a song written by Hezekiah Walker, *"Every Praise is to Our God."* Willie sang until his kidnapper let him go! I can shout right there.

The kidnapper cursed him and told him to shut up, but Willie kept singing these words, *"Every praise is to our God, every word of worship is to our God, Every Praise, Every Praise is to our God*!" The words of the song must have convicted the heart of the kidnapper because eventually, he kicked Willie out of the car. "He opened the door and threw me out," Willie said.

I wonder, this morning, when the enemy comes against you, do you revert to your training?

In your tragedy, do you have a song to sing? Are you willing to sing it until the enemy is so frustrated he gives up and walks away? I don't know what you're going through today, but I encourage you to keep singing, "Every Praise is to our God!" Keep singing until the enemy flees.

Personal Reflection

What daily whispers today remind you that you owe God praise?

_____

_____

_____

_____

_____

_____

_____

_____

_____

What does your daily praise look like? How can you improve it?

_____

_____

_____

_____

_____

_____

_____

_____

_____

_____

_____

Purpose

So many people wonder about their purpose in life.

The Wisdom Writer considered this question in Ecclesiastes and concluded we're all made for a specific purpose. He said, "After all this (studying life), there is only one thing to say: Have *reverence* for God and *obey* his commands because this is all that we were created for."

He concludes, no matter where we are or what we're doing, our purpose is to worship the true and living God.

Chapter 7

Whispers of Purpose

May I Take Your Order

"I am your God and will take care of you
until you are old and your hair is gray.
I made you and will care for you; I will
give you help and rescue you."

Isaiah 46:4

The other day my youngest son reminded me about an important lesson concerning confidence, faith, and trust. We happened to go to dinner with our extended family, so we had a large party. My son sat some distance away from me at the other end of the table. I noticed how he confidently opened his menu to place his order.

He never once checked with me. He never asked what he could order. He never asked what dad could afford, but he confidently made his request known to the server and waited on his order. You see, he had been through this before and innately knew if his father brought him to this place, his father would take care of him. His confidence made me smile.

Listen, I don't know what you're going through or what you'll face this year, but know this, if your Heavenly Father brought you to this place, your Father will take care of you. I encourage you to have the kind of faith, trust, and confidence that makes your Father smile because this is not the first time you've been here.

Keeper, Yes He Is!

"And my God will supply all your needs according to His riches in glory in Christ Jesus."

Philippians 4:19

I stumbled across a piece of paper the other day that reminded me just how good God has been to me. It was an old W-2 from the late 1990s, which showed my earnings for the year. I was shocked to learn I earned less than $15k that year because that little money doesn't match my memory.

How could this be? There must be some mistake. How in the world did we make it? I pulled up a military pay scale from the 1990s to double check this error because there was absolutely no way this was true...yet it was. I reflected on who we were at that time.

We were a young married couple with a small child. My wife was finishing her college degree. We had a child in day care and the usual bills of rent and a car loan, and of course we had to eat! My W-2 indicated we shouldn't have had much, but somehow, we had more than enough. We were never in want or in desperation.

As I look back, I can't even begin to explain it, but here's what I know: We kept God first, and he supplied all our needs. So, when you see me with my hands lifted and my eyes filled with tears it's because God's grace favored me. God's grace kept our marriage, the roof over our heads, and food on the table. I know firsthand that God is a keeper and I also know, if you trust Him, He'll keep you too.

A New Wardrobe

"If then God so clothes the grass, which today is in the field and tomorrow is thrown into the oven, how much more will He clothe you, O you of little faith?"

Luke 12:28

I don't know how my wife managed to mess up my laundry so badly, but somehow, she shrank EVERYTHING in my closet. It had to be a conspiracy. I tried on a pair of pants the other day, and there was absolutely no way I was getting in them. I tried on one thing after another and for some reason the woman I love messed up all my clothes. I looked into the closet at the end of the day and all I saw was a bunch of disappointed hangers waiting for something to hold.

It was a disappointing day. I could no longer fit into some things that had made me comfortable. However, somewhere in the middle of me trying on one disappointment after another, my wife snuck out of the house and bought me a few new things to fit the person I am today. I told you this was a conspiracy. She was kind enough to let me know I wasn't getting back into the things on the floor (Thank God for a good wife).

Well, life is a little like this. We're so busy trying to hold on to things that don't fit us anymore, and all the while God is trying to give us a brand-new wardrobe, but we refuse to let go of the old one. The enemy wants us to try to make ourselves small to fit into a wardrobe we've outgrown. Don't let the enemy keep you small but allow God to continue to expand His grace in you.

Let me be kind enough today to tell you bitterness and anger doesn't fit you anymore. Hatred and greed don't match the person you are today. When we wear things that don't fit, we make ourselves look foolish. Let God give you a brand-new wardrobe. Let Him clothe you in forgiveness. Let Him put righteousness on you. You'll look pretty darn good when you put on His joy, His peace, His kindness and top it off with His Love. I challenge you today to check your wardrobe. Are you still trying to wear something that doesn't fit the person you are today?

Permanent Change of Station (PCS)

"For we know that if the earthly tent we live
in is destroyed, we have a building from God, an
eternal house in heaven, not built
by human hands."

2 Cor 5:1

After 26 years of military service, my family and I are very experienced movers. We've lived in many places from Nebraska to Virginia. We've even lived overseas in places like Germany and Belgium. We knew that when we arrived in one place, it wouldn't be long until we received what are called Permanent

Change of Station (PCS) orders. I don't know how it worked at everyone else's house, but when we received our PCS orders, my wife started throwing "old stuff" out.

She would say stuff like, "We can't take that with us, or that's not going to fit in the new house." Please keep in mind, WE HAD NEVER BEEN TO THE PLACE WE WERE GOING, we didn't know where we would live, but my beautiful wife already knew that couch and those curtains wouldn't fit in the new house. She could visualize where we were going and knew we couldn't carry old stuff with us. So, every move, I found myself getting rid of "old stuff" so we could move to a new place (Somebody is going to get that in a minute).

I can hear my mother singing an old gospel song that goes something like this: "I moved from my old house, and I moved from my old friends, and I moved from my old way of life. Thank God I moved out, to a brand new life."

As Believers, we have PCS orders. We have Permanent Change of Spirit orders. We have Permanent Change of Salvation orders because our Savior has permanently changed us from the inside out. Our PCS orders declare that we're on our way to heaven, and that means we need to box up some old stuff and throw it out because it cannot go with us to the new place. Listen, your PCS orders are in, and it's time to move. You can't take that bitterness with you. You can't take that attitude with you. You can't take that anger with you. Throw it out, because it cannot go to the new place!

Divine Interruptions

*"**Now it happened**, the day after, that He went into a city called Nain; and many of His disciples went with Him, and a large crowd. And when He came near the gate of the city, **behold**, a dead man was being carried out, the only son of his mother; and she was a widow. And a large crowd from the city was with her."*

Luke 7:11-12

Has God ever interrupted your plans? Interruptions can be frustrating and upsetting. However, it just may be the needed delay to see the problem from another perspective, or the delay required to prevent you from saying the wrong thing at the wrong time.

I've come to appreciate God's Divine Interruptions because it is a display of His Compassion, Authority, and Power over my life. I've discovered the most meaningful events in my life were never on my agenda, but they were definitely on His.

I remember while on vacation in Nassau, Bahamas how my agenda was interrupted by His providential plan. God caused or allowed my path to intersect with someone struggling with a son at home, and somehow, through the conversation, I ended up praying for a stranger, in a strange place, in the middle of the street.

The question is how do you view these station identification moments in your life? For me, God's Divine Interruptions are just reminders that you still belong to him, and he has a purpose and plan for your life. Be blessed!

Step on the Scale

"Let Him weigh me with accurate scales, and let God know my integrity."

Job 31:6

I noticed a young man at the gym pull a scale out of his gym bag to weigh himself. The sight of him carrying a scale was a little odd to me because there were so many scales in the gym to weigh oneself. There was a look of disappointment on the young man's face when he did so, so I had to find out why.

As it turned out, he was a local high school wrestler and had a match that night. He was disappointed because after working out he was still two pounds over his weight limit and could be disqualified.

He carried his scale because he knew it was accurate, reliable, and the type used for the official weigh-in. He didn't want to use just any scale because he may not get a true reading. If he relied on someone else's scale, he could lose his match without ever stepping on the mat.

Have you ever disqualified yourself because you stepped on the wrong scale? We look pretty darn good when we weigh ourselves on our neighbor's, parent's, or friend's scale. However, when we step on God's scale, the one that is accurate, reliable, and the official weigh-in scale, we find we're still too heavy with sin. Whose scale are you using? I encourage you today to step on the right scale.

Unpack it!

"For God so loved the world that he gave his one and only Son, that whoever believes in him shall not perish but have eternal life."

John 3:16

My family and I, due to military commitments, have moved around the country several times. It is always interesting that for the first few days, even though we are in our house, it didn't feel like home because we hadn't unpacked yet. It's difficult to live and function amid chaos; we had to put things together and put some things in place for it feel like home. We needed to unpack. Over the years people have said to me, even though they've confessed faith, they still don't feel saved. I can honestly tell you, I know how you feel. I've had days like that myself. However, it's similar to our moves across the country, even though it didn't feel like home, we still signed the contract or the mortgage which made it our home. I'm so glad salvation doesn't depend on how we feel but it depends on our confession of faith (ownership).

Now that you have ownership…start unpacking. Unpack forgiveness, unpack hope, unpack love, unpack the strength needed to move to a new place in life, unpack the joy of your salvation, and you'll be able to function and even live in the midst of chaos. Don't live with your salvation boxed up. Unpack it!

Personal Reflections

What life purpose has God continued to reveal to you?

_____

_____

_____

_____

_____

_____

_____

_____

_____

_____

_____

_____

_____

_____

_____

_____

_____

_____

_____

_____

_____

What steps are you taking to move closer to fulfilling God's plan for your life?

_____

_____

_____

_____

_____

_____

_____

_____

_____

_____

_____

_____

_____

_____

_____

_____

_____

_____

_____

_____

_____

About the Author

Photo credit: Patrick Dean

Tracy Alan Barnett was born and raised in Erie, PA. Tracy was raised in a loving Christian home, by his mother Alice, and received the Lord as his savior at the age of seven. He is a proud graduate of Academy High School in Erie PA. He joined the United States Air Force immediately following high school and rose through the rank, and after 26 years of faithful serviced, retired as a Commissioned Officer.

He began ministry at the age of 19, and his service to the country allowed him to meet and share the Gospel with people across the country and many places around the world. For a year, he shared the gospel message in the war-torn country of Afghanistan and saw the power of God's word to sustain and encourage those in battle. Over the years, he has served in various capacities in many churches across the country.

He is now a Board-Certified Chaplain (BCC) specializing in Mental Health issues and serves as a Hospital Chaplain helping veterans recover from the trauma of war. He holds a Master of Divinity from Southwestern Baptist Theological Seminary, and a Master of Human Relations, from the University of Oklahoma. He also earned his undergrad in Management from the University of Maryland University College.

Closing Thoughts

God is intentional and everything that happens in our lives is a part of His plan, but we must open our spiritual ears to hear His voice.

I pray this book has encouraged you to seek God's hand in the small things that happen in your life every day. My deepest desire is that you develop the habit to listen for God's whispers in the morning.

If you know of someone who is struggling in one or more of the areas addressed in this book, would you be a blessing and recommend this book as a resource?

If you have any questions or comments, please feel free to reach out to me on Facebook @Whspr-Morn, or email: WhsprsMorn@gmail.com.

Looking for more devotions? Follow me on Facebook. I will periodically share new devotions there.

45862938R00075